MOVIE MAGIC
MAKEUP

BY SARA GREEN

BELLWETHER MEDIA • MINNEAPOLIS, MN

Blastoff! Discovery launches
a new mission: reading to learn.
Filled with facts and features, each
book offers you an exciting new
world to explore!

Library of Congress Cataloging-in-Publication Data

Names: Green, Sara, 1964- author.
Title: Makeup / by Sara Green.
Description: Minneapolis, MN : Bellwether Media, [2019]
   | Series: Blastoff! Discovery: Movie Magic | Includes
   bibliographical references and index.
Identifiers: LCCN 2018005004 (print) | LCCN 2018007336
   (ebook) | ISBN 9781626178489 (hardcover : alk. paper)
   | ISBN 9781681035895 (ebook)
Subjects: LCSH: Film makeup–Juvenile literature.
Classification: LCC PN1995.9.M25 (ebook) |
   LCC PN1995.9.M25 G74 2019 (print)
   | DDC 791.4302/7–dc23
LC record available at https://lccn.loc.gov/2018005004

Editor: Betsy Rathburn   Designer: Brittany McIntosh

Printed in the United States of America, North Mankato, MN.

TABLE OF CONTENTS

MAKEUP MARVELS!

The Avengers must fight for their lives! An evil robot named Ultron aims to destroy all humans on Earth. The character appears in the 2015 film *Avengers: Age of Ultron*. Only Iron Man, Thor, and the other Avengers can stop him.

Luckily, they have help. A new hero has joined the team. A robot named Vision is among them. Vision has a powerful Mind Stone. He uses it to help the Avengers defeat Ultron and his army!

VISION

THOR

Actor Paul Bettany plays Vision. It takes makeup artists around three hours to give Bettany his bold look. First, they put a cap on his head. It makes him look bald. Next, they glue **prosthetics** to his head and neck with **spirit gum**. Finally, the artists paint the actor's skin red.

The other actors wear makeup, too. **Foundation** and powder help keep their skin smooth and dry under bright lights. Makeup helps movies come to life!

GRUMPY AND GREEN

Jim Carrey played the Grinch in the 2000 film *How the Grinch Stole Christmas*. His makeup took about three hours to apply and one hour to remove each day!

WHAT IS MAKEUP?

Makeup is material applied to an actor's face or body in a film. It helps filmmakers tell a movie's story. It makes characters more believable for audiences. It also helps actors get into their roles. They look in a mirror and see their character looking back!

Makeup can be used for many purposes. Sometimes, it helps actors look much older. Special products may add wrinkles or change the skin's color. Other times, actors may play aliens, monsters, and other creatures. Makeup makes them look strange or scary!

THE NUTTY PROFESSOR

STAR WARS EPISODE I:
THE PHANTOM MENACE

9

Makeup artists use many types of makeup. Creams, powders, and other beauty products polish an actor's looks. **Special effects** makeup changes people's looks even more. Artists use **liquid latex** to make wrinkles. A special wax is often used to make scars.

Some characters have missing teeth. Makeup artists cover actors' teeth with black paint, wax, or caps. Makeup artists can also make actors look hairy. They use wool, human hair, or yak hair to make wigs and beards.

PIRATES OF THE CARIBBEAN: AT WORLD'S END

HISTORY OF MAKEUP

Makeup has always been a part of filmmaking. It started as stage makeup called **greasepaint**. But this heavy makeup was not easy to use. Its color and texture did not look natural in early black and white films.

In 1914, a man named Max Factor invented a new type of makeup. It was known as pancake makeup. Max's new makeup was lighter than traditional greasepaint. Movie stars wore it both on and off screen!

MAKEUP FOR ALL

Max Factor introduced Society Make-up in 1920. This was the first time the word "makeup" was used. Before that, beauty products were called cosmetics.

THE WIZARD OF OZ

Movie characters with unusual looks often needed special makeup. Filmmakers did not have **CGI** to create the effects. Instead, they relied on special effects makeup to get the right look.

A soft material called **foam latex** was introduced in the late 1930s. Makeup artists often used it to make masks. The 1939 film *The Wizard of Oz* was one of the first films to feature the makeup. It helped create the looks of the Cowardly Lion and the Scarecrow.

A FISHY PHANTOM

Actor Lon Chaney was known for playing scary characters in early films. Chaney often made his own makeup. He used putty, greasepaint, and fish skin to make himself into the Phantom for the 1925 film *The Phantom of the Opera*.

Over time, makeup techniques continued to improve. The makeup in a 1968 film called *Planet of the Apes* amazed audiences. Makeup artist John Chambers discovered a way to blend ape masks with the actors' skin. They could move their faces much more easily. This helped them show more expressions!

The **cast** included many actors playing apes. Chambers needed a large team of makeup artists. He taught them all how to make the actors look like real apes!

MOVIE MAKEUP PIONEER

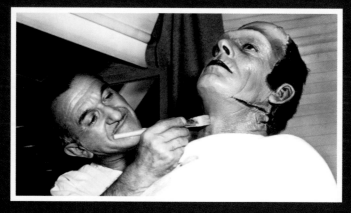

Name: Jack P. Pierce
Born: May 5, 1889, in Valdetsyou, Greece
Known For: Makeup artist who created famous makeup worn by Boris Karloff in *Frankenstein* (1931), as well as makeup in *The Mummy* (1932) and *The Wolf Man* (1941)
Awards: 2003 Lifetime Achievement Award from Hollywood Makeup Artist and Hair Stylist Guild

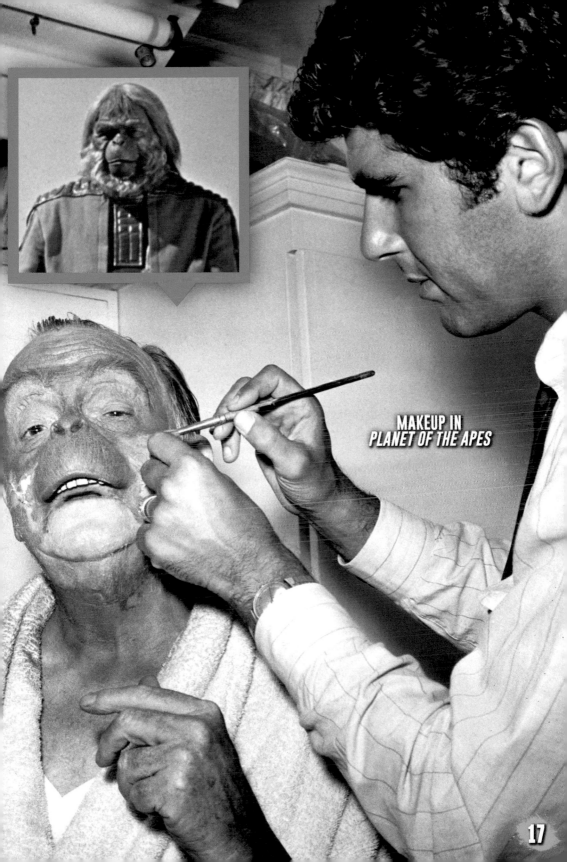

MAKEUP IN
PLANET OF THE APES

In the late 1960s, a makeup artist named Dick Smith began using foam latex in a new way. He layered small pieces on actors' faces. This helped the makeup look like real skin. It also gave actors more freedom to speak and show different emotions.

The 1970 movie *Little Big Man* brought much attention to Smith's new method. The actor playing the starring role was around 30 years old. But Smith made the character look like he was 121!

GOING UNDERCOVER

Foam latex pieces were also used in the 1993 film *Mrs. Doubtfire*. They helped transform actor Robin Williams into his family's housekeeper!

MAKEUP MAGIC

Over time, prosthetics have helped bring many unique characters to life. James McAvoy played a **faun** named Mr. Tumnus in the 2005 film *The Chronicles of Narnia: The Lion, the Witch and the Wardrobe*. McAvoy wore **silicone** ears. A remote-controlled device made them wiggle!

The actors who played hobbits in the Lord of the Rings film series wore prosthetic feet. Actor Johnny Depp wore hand prosthetics for his role in the 1990 movie *Edward Scissorhands*. The prosthetics looked like scissors!

THE CHRONICLES OF NARNIA: THE LION, THE WITCH AND THE WARDROBE

MODERN MOVIE MAKEUP ARTIST

Name: Bill Corso
Born: New Jersey
Known For: Makeup artist for more than 70 films, including *The Amazing Spider-Man* (2012) and *Star Wars: The Force Awakens* (2015)
Awards: 2005 Academy Award for *Lemony Snicket's A Series of Unfortunate Events*

LEMONY SNICKET'S A SERIES OF UNFORTUNATE EVENTS

DRAX

GAMORA

Bigger movies mean more movie makeup. The Guardians of the Galaxy film series has many characters with unique makeup looks. Zoe Saldana played an alien named Gamora. Makeup artists painted her face and body green. They added lines to her cheeks and forehead. Her eyebrows were also fake!

Actor Dave Bautista played Drax in the series. Artists put 18 different prosthetic pieces on his body. They also covered his body with tattoos and paint. Five makeup artists worked on him each day!

SPECIAL EFFECTS MAKEUP

Movie: *Wonder*
Year: 2017
Famous For: Actor Jacob Tremblay played a boy with a rare medical condition, requiring him to wear prosthetic makeup, including a device that pulled his lower eyelids down
Awards: Nominated for 2018 Academy Award for Best Makeup and Hairstyling

MAKEUP OR MONEY?

Some of the actors in *Black Panther* wear makeup that sparkles in the sun. A special powder in the makeup helps create that effect. The powder is used to make United States currency. Its glimmer proves the money is real.

Sometimes, makeup artists must use real people to inspire imaginary characters. Makeup artists for the 2018 movie *Black Panther* had to create looks for characters in a pretend African country called Wakanda. Real African **cultures** and **traditions** inspired the makeup artists.

They studied people across the **continent**. Then, they designed
face paintings, scars, and other looks for the movie characters.
Some characters even have **lip plates**! Makeup artists used
dental pieces and fake skin to create this look.

Today's makeup artists face new challenges. High-definition, or HD, movies have sharper images that show small details. Actors' makeup can look thick and unnatural.

To solve this problem, artists use makeup made especially for HD movies. It is thinner than other types of makeup. Many artists also use **airbrushing**. They blow makeup on actors' faces. This method blends makeup evenly into skin.

MANY USES

Airbrushing is used in many different ways. It adds details to makeup looks for TV shows, music videos, stage plays, and more!

MAKEUP AND CGI

Today, makeup and CGI are often used together. Editors use computers to add visual effects to actors' faces. This method was used to create Lord Voldemort's face in the Harry Potter film series. Makeup was applied to actor Ralph Fiennes' face. Then, CGI was used to flatten his nose to create a snakelike look.

However, many makeup artists still prefer doing makeup by hand. They enjoy the creative process and seeing results right away. Makeup magic helps bring characters to life!

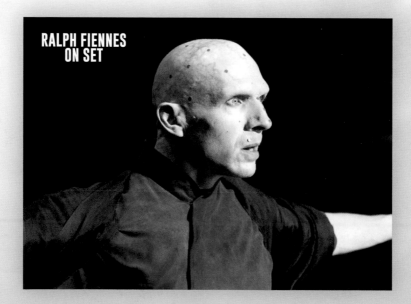

RALPH FIENNES
ON SET

VOLDEMORT
WITH CGI MAKEUP

GLOSSARY

airbrushing—a makeup method where artists use a special tool to blow a mixture of air and makeup onto an actor's face

cast—people who act in movies, plays, or other productions

CGI—artwork created by computers; CGI stands for computer-generated imagery.

continent—one of Earth's seven large land masses

cultures—the beliefs, arts, and ways of life in places or societies

faun—a pretend creature that is part human and part goat

foam latex—a soft, lightweight substance used to make masks and prosthetics

foundation—a skin-colored makeup applied to the face

greasepaint—a waxy substance actors used as makeup

lip plates—discs used to stretch the bottom lip, traditionally worn by some African and South American peoples

liquid latex—liquid rubber

prosthetics—fake body parts made from rubber or other materials

silicone—a flexible, rubbery substance made from a combination of chemicals

special effects—a misleading image created for movies by using makeup, special props, camera systems, computer graphics, and other methods

spirit gum—a glue used by makeup artists to attach prosthetics to people's faces and bodies

traditions—customs, ideas, and beliefs handed down from one generation to the next

TO LEARN MORE

AT THE LIBRARY

Hammelef, Danielle S. *Mind-Blowing Makeup in Special Effects*. North Mankato, Minn.: Capstone Press, 2015.

Horn, Geoffrey M. *Movie Makeup, Costumes, and Sets*. Milwaukee, Wis.: G. Stevens Pub., 2007.

Mason, Helen. *Makeup Artist*. New York, N.Y.: Gareth Stevens Publishing, 2015.

ON THE WEB

Learning more about makeup is as easy as 1, 2, 3.

1. Go to www.factsurfer.com.

2. Enter "makeup" into the search box.

3. Click the "Surf" button and you will see a list of related web sites.

With factsurfer.com, finding more information is just a click away.

INDEX

The images in this book are reproduced through the courtesy of: Entertainment Pictures/ Alamy, front cover, pp. 3, 20; Walt Disney Studios Motion Pictures/ Everett Collection, pp. 4, 4-5; Moviestore Collection Ltd/ Alamy, pp. 6, 19, 24; Marvel Studios/ Newscom, pp. 6-7; AF Archive/ Alamy, pp. 8, 8-9; James Fisher/ Warner Bros. Pictures/ Everett Collection, pp. 10-11; Buena Vista Pictures/ Everett Collection, p. 11; Ronald Grant Archive, p. 12; Everett Collection, pp. 12-13, 14-15, 15, 16; 20th Century Fox Film Corp./ Everett Collection, pp. 16-17, 17; Mary Evans/ Cinema Center Films/ Stockbridge-Hiller Productions/ Ronald Grant/ Everett Collection, pp. 18-19; Paramount/ Everett Collection, pp. 20-21; Splash News/ Alamy, p. 21; Chuck Zlotnick/ Walt Disney Studios Motion Pictures/ Everett Collection, pp. 22-23; ZUMA Press, Inc/ Alamy, p. 23; Matt Kennedy/ Marvel/ Walt Disney Studios Motion Pictures/ Everett Collection, pp. 24-25; Peter Lovino/ Universal Pictures/ Everett Collection, pp. 26-27; imageBROKER/ Alamy, p. 27; Warner Bros./ Everett Collection, pp. 28, 28-29.